Bobbie's Story

A Feelings Workbook

by Brennan Lynn Mars
Illustrated by D. H. Tsai
CWLA Press • Washington, DC

CWLA Press is an imprint of the Child Welfare League of America. The Child Welfare League of America (CWLA) is a privately supported, nonprofit, membership-based organization committed to preserving, protecting, and promoting the well-being of all children and their families. Believing that children are our most valuable resource, CWLA, through its membership, advocates for high standards, sound public policies, and quality services for children in need and their families.

CHILD WELFARE LEAGUE OF AMERICA, INC.
440 First Street, NW, Third Floor, Washington, DC 20001-2085
E-mail: books@cwla.org

CURRENT PRINTING (last digit)
10 9 8 7 6 5 4 3 2 1

Cover design by Jenny Geanakos
Cover illustration by D. H. Tsai

Printed in the United States of America

ISBN # 0–87868-735-1

Professional Disclaimer

Due to the subject matter of *Bobbie's Story*, the author recommends that her materials not be used without the guidance of a treatment professional. Should you obtain a copy of the workbook and/or foster parent guide, please consult the child's social worker or therapist to help you in using these materials.

This is my book.

This is a story about Bobbie—that's me!

I am eight years old.

I live with my foster parents, Betty and Jim.

What is your name?
How old are you?
What are the names of your foster parents?

My name is____________________________.

I am ____________ years old.

My foster mother's name is ____________________.

My foster father's name is _____________________.

I came to live with Betty and Jim
because of what Sam did.
For a long time nobody knew
what was happening to me.
Sam told me to keep it a secret.
It is hard for me to talk about
what happened.
Sometimes it helps me to talk
to my foster parents.

Sometimes I feel sad.
I feel that it is all my fault.
Sam told me that if someone found out,
it would break up my family.
Betty and Jim say, “It is not your fault.
You were not safe living with your family.”

Sometimes I feel bad,
because I played games with Sam.
I didn't want to stop.
Betty and Jim say, "It is not your fault.
Sam should not have asked you
to play those kind of games."

Sometimes I feel bad,
because I liked it when Sam touched me.
I felt like Sam's special friend.
I got special toys from Sam.
Betty and Jim say, "It is not your fault.
You are very special to us.
In our house, grown-ups do not touch
children's private parts."

Sometimes I feel bad,
because I didn't tell sooner.
Sometimes I feel that
I should have been able to stop Sam.
Betty and Jim say, "It is not your fault.
Sam is a grown-up and should have known better."

Many people have told me
that what Sam did was wrong.
Grown-ups call it sexual abuse.
Sometimes I feel dirty and ashamed.
Betty and Jim say, “You are wonderful.
You are not dirty. It is not your fault.”

I have many feelings about what happened.
Maybe you do too.

ANGER

Sometimes I feel **angry** at my mommy.
My mommy didn't believe me.
My mommy didn't protect me.
Sometimes I feel **angry** at Sam for
what happened to me.
Sometimes I feel **angry** because
I had to move away from my home.
Sometimes I feel **angry** because people keep
making me tell my story over and over.

What things make you **angry**?

Draw a picture of your **angry** feelings.

Use extra sheets of paper if you need to.

SAD

Sometimes I feel **sad,**
because my mommy didn't believe me.
Sometimes my mommy was not there
to take care of me.
Sometimes I feel **sad,**
because I had to leave my family,
home, friends, and school.
Sometimes I feel **sad,**
because Sam had to go to jail.

What things make you **sad**?

Draw a picture of your **sad** feelings.
Use extra sheets of paper if you need to.

LOTS OF DIFFERENT FEELINGS

Sometimes I don't know how to feel.
I have lots of different feelings.
I don't know if I can trust anyone.
I love my parents, but I am angry at them.
I feel better in my new home,
but I miss my other home.

What are the **different kinds of feelings** that you have?

Draw a picture of the **different kinds of feelings** that you have.

Use extra sheets of paper if you need to.

SCARY FEELINGS

Sometimes I am **afraid** of Betty and Jim.

I am careful to be nice.

But sometimes I get so angry.

I am **afraid** of what Jim and Betty might do.

What things make you **afraid**?

Draw a picture of **scary** feelings.

Use extra sheets of paper if you need to.

Sometimes I feel like I can’t do anything right.
Sometimes school is hard.
Sometimes I feel that nobody likes me at school.
Sometimes I feel like giving up.

Betty and Jim's home is different
than my other home.

Betty and Jim have rules about
how adults and children behave.
Betty and Jim talk about good touching
and bad touching.
Good touches make me feel happy and warm.
Bad touches make me feel uncomfortable.

Betty and Jim said that sometimes grown-ups may need to help children put medicine on their private parts if they have a rash.

Sometimes grown-ups may need to help young children wash their private parts. Sometimes a doctor may have to look at a child's private parts.

Still, it isn't OK for grown-ups to play with children's private parts.

Betty and Jim said it isn't OK for children to touch a grown-up's private parts. They also said that it isn't OK for children to touch other children's private parts.

Betty and Jim say that everyone must knock
before going into someone's bedroom
or the bathroom.

Betty and Jim help me learn what to say if someone tries to touch my private parts or if someone asks me to touch another person's private parts.

I can say,
"No, don't touch me! I don't like it!"
"No, I won't touch you! I don't like it!"

Then I can go tell a grown-up that I trust.
I could tell Betty and Jim, or I could tell a teacher.

Betty and Jim say that our bodies are special.

My body belongs only to me.
Your body belongs only to you.

People cannot touch my body,
unless I say that it's OK.

About the Author and the Illustrator

Brennan Lynn Mars, Psy.D., conducts family therapy, play therapy, couples and marital therapy, parenting skills training; provides crisis intervention; and administers psychodiagnostic tests to children at the Julia Ann Singer Center in Los Angeles, California. She received her doctorate in Clinical Psychology with an individual/family/child proficiency from the California School of Professional Psychology in Los Angeles.

Daniel H. Tsai is Art Director/Graphic Designer for his company, Anarchy, in Glendale, California.

About Bobbie's Story . . .

by
Brennan Lynn Mars

Bobbie's Story: A Feelings Workbook tells the story of a young child who was sexually abused and is now living with foster parents. It is designed to be read together by the child and foster parent, once foster parents have received appropriate guidance and training.

Bobbie's Story: A Guide for Foster Parents (sold separately) provides foster parents with information about the sexual abuse of children, resulting behavior and feelings, and suggestions for working with abused children as they deal with their experiences. The *Guide* is divided into sections that correspond with pages in the *Workbook*: self-blame (and how others view sexual abuse), betrayal, powerlessness, adjusting to new rules, and empowering the sexually abused child.

To order additional copies of *Bobbie's Story: A Feelings Workbook*		
1999/0-87868-735-1	Stock #7351	$5.95

To order *Bobbie's Story: A Guide for Foster Parents*		
1999/0-87868-701-7	Stock #7017	$12.95

Write: CWLA
P.O. Box 2019
Annapolis Junction, MD 20701-2019
E-mail: cwla@pmds.com

Call: 800/407-6273
301/617-7825
Fax: 301/206-9789

Bulk discount policy (not for resale): 10-49 copies 10%, 50-99 copies 20%, 100 or more copies 40%. Canadian and foreign orders must be prepaid in U.S. funds. MasterCard/Visa accepted.